THE [illegible]

Illustrated by Stephen Millingen

ANGLIA *young* BOOKS

First published in 1990
by Anglia Young Books
Durhams Farmhouse, Ickleton
Saffron Walden, Essex CB10 1SR

Reprinted 1993

Illustrations by Stephen Millingen

British Library Cataloguing in Publication Data
Swallow, Su
The haunted coast.
I. Title
823.914 [J]

ISBN 1–871173–10–8

Typeset in Palatino
and printed in Great Britain by
Redwood Books

For Jon, Matheu and Ben

AUTHOR'S NOTE

Dunwich is a small village on the Suffolk coast, surrounded by meadows, marshes, heathland and forest. In medieval times, however, Dunewic was a busy market town and port, with a population of about 4,000. So how did the town disappear?

Then, as now, it was a place that the sea would never leave alone. The coastline has been eroded to such an extent that, today, the once-thriving Dunewic is nothing but ruins beneath the water.

What was life like in medieval Dunewic? In THE HAUNTED COAST, Felix meets all kinds of local people, from a poor fisherman to a rich merchant. He joins the townspeople in their battle against the sea, and fights his own battle against a band of pirates.

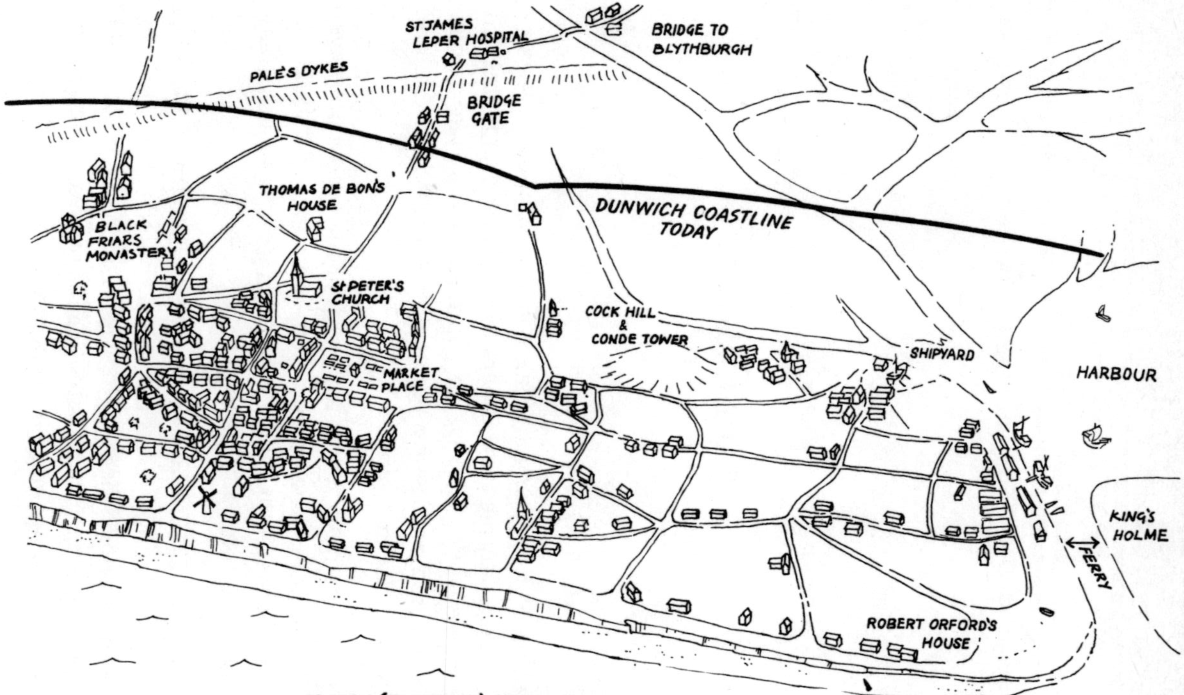

DUNWICH (DUNEWIC) AS IT WAS IN 1285

CHAPTER ONE

The boy walked slowly down the village street – past the church, the tiny museum with its lattice windows, and the Ship Inn. He turned left at the end and faced the sea wind. He shivered and pushed his hands into his jacket pockets, sliding and stumbling over the pebbles as he skirted round the fishing boats pulled up on the beach. Felix was tired after the long walk from his grandfather's house. He sat down on the stones, his back against a dinghy, and took a sandwich out of his pocket.

Why did this place feel so familiar, he wondered. He was a stranger in Dunwich – this was his first visit. But in some peculiar way he knew it. Not as it was now, this tiny village. Somewhere in his mind there was a picture of a much bigger place, a busy port with a market and noise and bustle. He closed his eyes and images began to form – images of sailing galleys and shipyards, and crowds of jostling, shouting people selling their wares at market. He could even smell the fish drying in the wood smoke . . . Felix tried to shake off the dream. Briefly, he opened his eyes and they rested on the name of the dinghy, DONEWYC.

DONEWYC! Was that the name of the place he knew? Dunewic? Donmoc? Yes, that was it. Not Dunwich. He closed his eyes again and the pictures became more and more real until at last they took substance and he found himself in among the jostling crowds . . . but this was still not quite how he remembered Donmoc. It still wasn't his time – not yet – not quite yet.

• • • • •

Felix blinked in the bright sun. He found himself standing by the quayside, looking down on a row of small wooden fishing boats that tipped and swayed gently on the muddy water of the harbour. Beyond them, against the sun, stood the dark shapes of wide sailing galleys and heavy barges. Men were busy loading and unloading the ships, filing up and down the ramps with crates and barrels, and shouting instructions to each other.

A young man in a long crimson robe stood counting casks of wine as they were lifted off the *Selig*, a wide-bodied sailing ship whose stem and stern rose up sharply to give it a U shape. The man shouted at the men to hurry, as he checked the numbers of casks on his counting board. Felix moved closer to read the chalk marks on the wooden casks. Gascogne, 1285. Felix frowned. What did the figure mean? The price? The quantity? He gasped as he realised the truth: it was the year. He was in a medieval port! 'What is going on?' he cried. As he spoke, the man in crimson turned and stared at him.

'Don't spy, boy. It won't do you any good,' he hissed. Felix jumped back nervously. He wondered what he was spying on, but felt it safer to move away. Where should he go? Who could he ask? He looked around at all the strange faces and was surprised at how lost and lonely he felt in this busy crowd. He was used to being on his own and coping by himself. He must make a plan. First, he had to find out where he was. If this *was* his Donmoc,

then he knew there was a good viewing post nearby, a lookout tower on the hill. He made his way past a little church and down a very narrow cobbled lane, standing sideways to let other people pass him. Yes. There was the little hill, rising above most of the surrounding cottages, with a wooden tower standing on the flat top. He would climb up and get his bearings. Then he would have to decide what to do.

Felix scrambled up the steep sandy slope to the foot of the tower, then climbed on, up the wooden ladders to the top. The wind tore at his hair and clothes and made him catch his breath. He clung to the rail, shaded his eyes and looked slowly round at the scene below. The extent of the town was marked out on three sides by a rampart topped by a wooden palisade. On the fourth side lay the sea. Beyond the town wall lay flat marshes, fields of crops and forests. Below him, a busy harbour, shipyards, warehouses and hundreds of thatched roofs crowded together, some on the flat ground close to the sea and others, some quite large, important-looking houses, stretching up the higher part of the town. Windmills and grey stone churches stood in open spaces scattered through the town. So many churches, thought Felix, as he counted the spires and towers – eight, nine, ten . . . He felt again that strange feeling of knowing this place, and what is more, of belonging. He looked again at the town, searching for another church. A small, wooden church, by the sea. The picture in his mind was sharp, but he could not find it.

'You're a stranger in Dunewic, aren't you?'

Felix jumped in fright as a voice close by him broke into his thoughts. He turned and saw a boy in brown tunic and leggings standing behind him.

'No . . . er, well yes, I suppose I am,' said Felix lamely, knowing he could not explain how he felt. The other boy stared at him suspiciously.

'What are you doing up here? Are you spying?'

'No of course not. I wanted to work out where I was and what to do.'

'Well, I've got real work to do. Move over.'

The boy moved to the rail and stared out to sea. He stood very still, concentrating. Felix did not like to disturb him.

'Yes, there they are. Look!'

Felix looked but did not see anything.

'There, on the horizon,' said the boy impatiently. 'The gulls.'

'So what?' asked Felix, then wished he hadn't sounded so challenging. 'I mean, why are the gulls so special?'

'You *are* a stranger here if you don't know that,' said the boy, full of scorn. 'The gulls follow the herrings. We fish for herrings. The gulls tell us when and where to fish. I must go and tell my father.' As the boy explained, Felix looked past him and saw the birds clearly now, a ragged white cloud that kept reshaping itelf over the glistening water.

The boy rushed past Felix to the top of the ladder. Perhaps his eyes were blinded by the sun. Perhaps the wind caught him off balance. As he turned to go down the ladder, his foot missed the first rung. He cried out, and tried to grasp the upright support, but he could not save himself. Felix could do nothing as the boy fell away from the ladder. Seconds later the boy landed in an awkward heap at the base of the tower. Felix climbed down as fast as he dared. He crouched down by the boy, who lay white-faced with fear and pain.

'I can't move,' he said in a whisper. Felix tried to stay calm, although he felt frightened too. Was the boy badly hurt? He had seemed rough – almost rude – in the tower. Now he seemed helpless. Felix felt sorry for him.

'I'll fetch help. Tell me who you are and where you live,' said Felix. The boy tried to move his arm and cried out with pain.

'My name is Robert,' he said quietly. 'I live in St Leonard's parish, close to the harbour mouth. Ask for the house of John Orford the fisherman. He is my father. Please hurry,' said Robert, biting back the tears.

Felix unpinned his cloak – accepting his change into medieval clothes without surprise – and tucked it round Robert. 'If I leave you my cloak, you know I will return,' said Felix. Then he slid down the hill and ran in the direction of the sea.

• • • • •

'Is this the house of John Orford?' Felix had been directed

to a small thatched cottage at the end of a narrow lane. The cottage stood close to the sea, separated from the sea wall only by a small vegetable plot and a fenced area where two pigs and a few chickens were feeding on some kitchen scraps. Felix took all this in at a glance and turned back to the low, dark doorway to the cottage. A tall man with a dark, weatherbeaten face was stacking wicker baskets.

'What if it is John Orford's house?' the man asked warily, wearing the same suspicious frown as Felix had seen on his son's face earlier. 'Who wants to know?'

'I'm . . . Felix, a stranger in your town, but I know your son Robert. He needs help. He's fallen from the tower.'

'The tower? The conde on Cock Hill, you mean? Dear God, is he badly hurt? What happened?'

'I don't know – he was too frightened to try moving.'

'We must hurry, then. Come on.'

They carried Robert home and laid him on a straw mattress in the far room of the little two-room cottage. Nobody took any notice of Felix, who stood back in the gloom, waiting to see if the boy was going to be all right. 'No bones broken, thank God,' said Robert's father at last. 'You've got some nasty bruises, and that shoulder will take a while to recover. It's badly sprained, but your mother will prepare a poultice to take the swelling down. You'll mend, don't worry,' he said, smiling with relief. 'Now, whatever made you fall? You go up and down the tower nearly every day.'

Robert sat up suddenly, the pain from his shoulder making him gasp.

'Father – the gulls – they're about five miles out, directly to the east. We must go now. It will be a big catch, I know.'

'You'll have to miss this one, I'm afraid,' replied his father, 'you couldn't pull the oars with that shoulder.'

'But *you* must go, father. We promised to send ten baskets of fresh herring to the monastery before Easter, and that's next week.'

John Orford nodded.

'You're right, boy,' he said. 'I must go at once. Now, rest and get well. I need you to be fit and strong as soon as possible.'

Felix frowned as he listened to this exchange. He felt responsible in some way for the accident, and wanted to prove he was no spy.

'Sir, I think I might be able to help you, if you will let me,' began Felix. John Orford turned round in surprise.

'Felix, I had forgotten you were still there. What is this idea of yours?' he asked, looking hard at Felix as though he were trying to decide whether to trust him.

'Well, I know nothing of fishing, but I'm not afraid of the sea. Why don't I take Robert's place on the oars?'

The man looked from Felix to his son and back again.

'There seems no reason not to trust you, boy. You helped

to rescue my son and seem to care about him. And it is true that a good catch today would help us a great deal. I accept your offer of help. What do you think, Robert?'

'I think you must go quickly,' said Robert, looking relieved. 'Thank you, Felix. I am sorry if I was unfriendly to you before, but it's like that with strangers, you know.'

'I'm not really a stranger' began Felix, but before he could explain any further, Robert's father was hurrying him out of the cottage. 'Come along, Felix. You can start helping straightaway. Put all these baskets and nets together while I go and tell the other fishermen. From what Robert has said, there will be enough for us all.'

• • • • •

Robert had been right. It was a good catch. Felix had helped the rest of Orford's crew to haul the nets up into the boat, full of silver herring that thrashed and slapped against each other, filling the boat with the smell of the sea. They and the other boats were ready to make for home as the sun began to set. Robert's mother met them at the quayside and helped them to unload the fish. People from the town crowded round to buy fresh fish for their supper. Felix, very tired but determined not to give up, helped to fetch huge wicker baskets from the smoke house, where a few fishermen were already busy cleaning their catch and threading the fish onto wooden skewers ready to smoke them over the log fire that burned slowly in the middle of the floor. He liked the smell of fish and smoke that clung to the baskets, which they lined with fresh straw before filling them with some of the freshly-caught herring, ready for the monks at the monastery.

Felix was suddenly aware of someone looking at him. He glanced up. The young man in the crimson robe, who had called him a spy that morning, was scowling at him. Felix shivered and looked away quickly, but his thoughts were interrupted by John Orford.

'The Black Friars will be well pleased with this gift,' he said. 'We have kept our promise to them, thanks to you, Felix. We can offer you a night's lodging in return for your help – and a good herring or two for supper, of course!' So Felix went back to the fisherman's cottage and recounted every detail of his fishing trip to Robert, whose mother meanwhile prepared a thick vegetable soup and baked herring.

'You make the work sound very exciting!' said Robert, laughing at his new friend's enthusiasm.

'It was exciting for me,' said Felix. 'Perhaps I will write it down while it is still fresh in my mind – but not tonight. I'm too tired.'

'Write it down?' asked Robert. 'Can you write, then?'

'Of course, can't you?'

'Fishing folk don't go to school. Surely you know that? You *are* a stranger here, aren't you? You must come from very far away. Where exactly do you come from?

'Well I ... it's rather difficult ...' Felix mumbled unhappily.

'Does your family know where you are?' asked Robert's mother after a pause.

'My parents are both dead,' said Felix, looking at the floor.

'Who looks after you, then?'

'No one. There's just me.'

No one spoke for a while.

'Well, we'd better look after you for now, then,' said Robert's mother gently. 'Time for bed, I think. We can talk again tomorrow.'

Felix looked at her. Had she believed him? How could he explain, when he felt so confused himself? Perhaps everything would be clearer in the morning. He said goodnight and lay down on a lumpy straw mattress on the earth floor. He soon learned to ignore the scuffling sounds of the mice and the strong smell of smoke from the fire. Tomorrow he would have to find a job, he thought, as he closed his eyes.

• • • • •

In the end, he did not need to look for a job until after Easter. He stayed with Robert's family and went out fishing with John Orford until Robert's arm was strong enough for him to row again. Then one day, John Orford said he must speak to him about the future.

'You're a good worker, Felix,' he said. 'I am sorry that we cannot afford to keep you with us now that Robert is better, but I can help you find a good place. Thomas de

Bon is looking for a new clerk, an honest boy who can read and write, and one who likes the sea. I'll take you to him tomorrow if you like.'

Felix thanked John Orford for his kind offer. Later, he asked Robert about Thomas de Bon.

'Master Thomas? He's a merchant. He owns three galleys. The *Selig* is one of his – it was in the harbour the day you arrived. I think it had just returned from France with its load of wine from Gascony.'

'What is Master Thomas like?' asked Felix nervously, remembering the suspicious young man in the red robe who had called him a spy.

'He's quite old now, and well respected in the town. Quite rich, too. No family – his son was drowned last year on the way to France. His ship was caught in a storm.'

'The next one will be far worse,' said Felix suddenly, as a picture of another, terrible storm came into focus in his mind.

Robert looked at him oddly, but just said,

'What do you mean?'

'Nothing.' And Robert had to be content, once again, with an anxious smile and shrug of the shoulders that his friend often gave instead of explanation.

CHAPTER TWO

Thomas de Bon took on Felix as his clerk for an annual wage of £13 plus board and lodging. He lived, like the other wealthy merchants of the town, in a large, two-storey manor house of flint and oak, built on the high ground away from sea. Only the poor people of Dunewic – the fishermen and farmworkers – lived on the low ground near the shore, where the high tides and winter storms often combined to flood the little cottages and even, on occasion, to sweep them away into the water.

Felix liked Master Thomas, who seemed quieter and gentler than many of the merchants who met and traded on the quay and in the market square every day. He seemed, indeed, rather sad. Felix remembered what had had happened to his son in the shipwreck.

'I'll show you the store room and tell you about your duties,' said Master Thomas. 'When my assistant comes back from the market, he can take you down to the warehouses in the harbour.'

Felix followed his new master across the stone floor of the huge hall, the main room of the house. The dark oak panelling and the heavy wool tapestries, the massive oak table flanked by long benches, the beautifully carved chair at the end, two chests with iron clasps – the room was simply but richly furnished. As Felix looked around, contrasting his new home with Robert's simple cottage with its mud and straw walls, and the animals sheltering under the same roof, he suddenly spotted something that delighted him. There, on a deep stone window sill, was a chess set, ivory figures arranged on a wooden chequer board. Felix stopped to admire them.

'Can you play chess?' asked Thomas de Bon.

'Not very well, Master Thomas, but these figures are beautiful.'

'Yes. My son carved them.' Thomas de Bon fell silent and Felix did not know how break the silence. Suddenly they were both startled by another voice.

'The *Selig* will be ready to sail tomorrow, Master Thomas, if the wind is set right.'

Felix felt goose pimples spread over his skin, and his heart thumped hard in his chest. He knew without looking who had spoken, but hoped desperately that he was wrong. It was the rasping voice of the young man at the harbour, the one who had told him not to spy.

'Ah, Ralph. Felix is our new clerk.' He turned to Felix. 'This is my assistant,' he explained. 'As you're back, Ralph, you can show Felix round and settle him in. He can start work this afternoon.' Master Thomas took a heavy iron key from his belt and opened the door to the store room. Ralph frowned but said nothing. Instead, he led the way into the store. Felix followed him, wondering how he was going to work with this man who seemed to dislike him so much.

It was cold and musty in the store. The light came in through two small windows high up on one wall, their criss-crossed iron bars casting strange patterns on the opposite wall. Ralph watched as Felix gazed about him.

'If you got shut in here,' whispered Ralph, 'no one would hear you. Remember that. Just do as I tell you and don't interfere in my work,' he said. Was he threatening Felix in some way? Why was he so hostile? What did he have to hide? Felix tried hard to concentrate as Ralph described the goods in the store: salt and wine from Gascony, furs, woven cloth from Flanders, whale oil . . .

'Are you paying attention, boy?'

'Yes, yes,' said Felix nervously.

'Well I can't stay here. It's time I went back to check on the *Selig*. Perhaps the sea air will wake you up. You'll have to come with me, I suppose,' said Ralph, leading the way out of the house and down the hill to the harbour. Felix was given parchment, quill and ink and told to make a note of every sack of wool that was taken from the warehouse to be loaded on to the *Selig*. He watched as the wool was weighed on a huge wooden weighbeam. The customs man worked out the tax due on Master Thomas's sacks of wool which were being sent to the weavers in Flanders, across the North Sea.

'Keep a check,' barked Ralph at Felix. 'It's 7s 6d a sack. Don't let him overcharge us.'

The customs man glanced at Ralph but said nothing.

Felix felt happier now that he had a job to do and for the rest of the day he tried hard to please the merchant's irritable assistant.

That evening, after supper in the kitchen, Felix was told to take some ale up to Master Thomas, who was sitting by a log fire in a small upstairs room. The merchant asked Felix about his first day, then asked him if he would like to play chess. Felix was surprised and pleased. He went down to the long hall to fetch the chess set. When the pieces were set up, they cast strange shadows on the board in the candlelight. Felix soon became absorbed in the game, and in the stories Master Thomas told him about the countries he had sailed to for trade, and about his son lost at sea.

When he went to bed, in a room on the ground floor at one end of the house, he found Ralph already there. Neither of them were happy about having to share the same room, but Felix hoped that the situation might get better if he continued to work hard.

'So, we can play chess, can we?' Ralph said in greeting. 'Cosy chats with the Master on your first day here. I knew you were a spy. If I catch you interfering in my business, you'll swing from the top of the weighbeam. Now, go to sleep and don't disturb me.' They both pulled off their leather boots and lay down, but Felix felt too cold and miserable to sleep. He lay very still, trying to understand

Ralph's anger. He remembered a look he had seen several times in Ralph's eyes. It was a look more of fear than anger, thought Felix, as though Ralph felt threatened by Felix.

A door creaked. It was their door! Felix peered into the

darkness and saw Ralph leaving by the door that led straight into the street. Felix sat up, then, on an impulse, he got out of bed, pulled on his boots and slipped out of the door. Ralph was still in view and, keeping to the shadows, Felix followed him. If Ralph did not want Felix to 'interfere', he might be plotting a crime of some sort, and Felix felt safer doing something than waiting for the unkown to happen.

The town was quiet but for the roar of the sea as it endlessly dragged the pebbles down the shore and then threw them back again.Felix walked into the wind and tugged his cloak tight around him, but it did little to keep out the cold. He hurried down the lane, his soft boots slipping on the wet cobbles. Then he stopped and held his breath. Ralph had reached the door of St Peter's Church. He looked round quickly, did not see Felix, then crept inside. Felix waited. What was Ralph doing? Not praying, of that Felix was sure. Then Ralph reappeared, carrying a leather bag over his shoulder, and set off down Bridge Street.

Why is he leaving the town, and under cover of darkness? thought Felix. He followed Ralph carefully as far as Bridge Gate, where the main street crossed Pales Dyke, the wooden fence that protected the town. The assistant strode over the bridge that ran over the deep ditch on the far side of the fence. Felix hesitated. He had never been outside the town since his mysterious arrival before Easter. Few people moved far from their home town for fear of robbers and bandits, and in any case, Felix knew that this road led to the leper hospital. He had heard terrible stories about how disfigured and crippled some of the lepers were, and did not want to go near.

As he hesitated, the countryside was suddenly flooded in moonlight and Felix had a clear view of what was happening ahead of him. Ralph had met two men on horseback, and was handing over the bag to them. Felix stared, then was startled by an eerie sound close by. A dark, hooded figure, swinging a bell on a chain, was coming towards him. A leper with his warning bell. Felix forgot all about Ralph in an instant, and turned and fled back to the town gate. Clouds blacked out the moon, and in the sudden darkness Felix stumbled and fell, not to the ground but down into a deep pit. Pales Dyke ditch was not easy to get out of – its purpose was, after all, to stop unwelcome visitors attacking the town – but Felix finally dragged himself up by clinging to woody, thorn-spiked stems of the wild rose and bramble that smothered the sides of the ditch.

• • • • •

The next morning, Felix was woken early by the sound of horns. He went to the hall to find out what was going on. But before he got to the doorway, he heard Ralph shouting, followed by the quieter voice of Master Thomas. Then more shouting. Did Ralph know that Felix had followed him? Was he telling Master Thomas? Felix stopped and listened.

' . . . and get rid of *him*. I don't need anyone to help me,' growled Ralph.

'He will be good company for me. My son . . .'

'Your son,' snarled Ralph. 'Your son was a scoundrel, an owler. If you don't keep your promise to me, I will tell the town all about your son. Your reputation as an honest merchant will be worth nothing then.'

'What you say is not true, as you must know. But you also know that I have not been able to discover where my goods disappeared to or who was responsible. Until I have proof of the real culprit, I do not want my son's name tarnished with any of this. If you stay quiet I will keep my promise to you – you will take over from me when I am too old to sail to foreign ports. Are you satisfied?' Master Thomas sounded resigned.

'What guarantee do I have now? If Felix stays you might adopt him as your son. Then he will want all this.'

'Leave Felix out of this,' said Master Thomas angrily. 'I have given you my word. That has always been good enough. Now leave me in peace. Go and call the boy. It's time for work.'

'Very well. But just remember . . .' Ralph strode to the open doorway. 'FELIX!' he shouted. Felix waited a few seconds before going in, trying to look calm and hiding his thorn-scratched hands in his wide sleeves.

'You are pale,' said Master Thomas. 'Did you not sleep well? Are you ill?'

Ralph looked at him sharply but Felix tried to ignore him. 'I am quite well, thank you Master Thomas. I woke early because of the horns. What did they mean?'

'Haymaking starts today. The horns call all hands to the

fields. You can go, after the *Selig* has sailed with the tide this morning.' Master Thomas rose from his chair. 'Let's go down to the port together.'

The *Selig* was ready. The last barrels of fresh drinking water, dark loaves of newly-baked bread and baskets of smoked herrings were among the last items to be loaded, enough to feed the fifty-man crew on their journey across the North Sea. Felix thought it strange that Master Thomas sold the fleeces of wool to Flemish merchants, who hired weavers to turn it into beautiful cloth which they would bring back to Dunewic to sell to other merchants in the market. But however strange, Felix envied the sailors.

'I would like to sail in her one day, Master Thomas,' he said.

'To Flanders?'

'No, home to France,' said Felix, without thinking. Why had he said that, he wondered. Was France home? He tried to picture it.

'Wake up, Felix,' cried Master Thomas. 'Stop dreaming! I was asking if you came from France.'

'Felix!' cried Robert. 'I knew I would find you here.'

Felix was glad Robert had suddenly appeared. He knew he could not explain his yearning to sail to France; he did not understand it himself. Once again, he smiled, shrugged his shoulders and said nothing.

Robert had come to see if Felix could go to the fields for

the haymaking. Master Thomas told Felix he was free for the rest of the day. 'Perhaps the sun will give you back some colour,' he said. 'I will go home with Ralph.' Ralph, however, had vanished without a word. The two boys watched as Thomas de Bon made his lonely way back along the quay and up towards the market square.

• • • • •

The boys found they were not really needed in the fields either.

'I know. Let's go to Kings Holme,' suggested Robert. The marshy wasteland across the harbour had become a favourite place for the two boys ever since Robert had taken Felix there to collect birds' eggs at Easter. They went to find the ferryman, who rowed them across for a halfpenny each.

'You'd best keep an eye out for trouble,' he warned. They say the men from Blythburgh are in angry mood again.'

Trouble often flared up between the men of Dunewic and men from Blythburgh and the other villages up the river. Their ships all had to use Dunewic harbour to reach the sea, and the men resented having to pay the harbour taxes. Other fights broke out over who owned shipwrecks that washed up on Kings Holme beach. It was best not to get in the way of such fights, and the boys thanked the ferryman for his advice.

Today, the marsh seemed empty and still as they walked barefoot over the spiky grass and through large clumps of golden samphire and pale mauve sea lavender. Sometimes they sank ankle-deep into the cold, rust-coloured water of the marsh. When they reached the dunes, they lay back against the sun-warmed sand, drying their feet and watching the gulls and terns wheeling overhead.

Felix broke the silence.

'What's an owler?' he asked.

'An owler?' Robert frowned. 'Don't you know anything? It's a merchant who exports wool secretly without paying the tax on it. Owlers work at night, like the owls. Why do you want to know?'

'I overheard Ralph talking about them,' said Felix, who did not want to explain everything just yet.

'Ralph? I wouldn't be surprised if he was one,' said Robert. 'But it's very difficult to catch them.' They both fell silent again.

'Race you to the top!' cried Robert suddenly, and set off up the dune slope, pushing sand down into Felix's face with every step. When they reached the top, each claiming victory, they saw that they were not alone on their wasteland after all. Down on the pebble beach, leaning against an old barge, sat a group of men, drinking ale and talking.

'Come on, let's go before they see us,' said Robert. 'They look like the Blythburgh gang. They're not Dunewic folk, anyway. And look, they've got cross bows.'

'Wait!' whispered Felix, dropping down on to his stomach and peering through the tall marram grass at the men below.

'Are you sure they're not from Dunewic?' he asked.

'Yes, why?'

'Because I recognise two of them. I saw them last night at the bridge to Blythburgh.'

'Last night?' gasped Robert. 'You were outside the town? And you talk of owlers. What is going on?'

Felix hesitated. Should he tell Robert about Ralph? Felix decided he could do nothing by himself, but perhaps with Robert's help they could find out what Ralph was up to. So he told Robert about how unpleasant Ralph had been, about the midnight meeting, the church, the argument this morning. They had nearly reached the ferry by the time he had finished.

'I am worried for Master Thomas,' said Felix. 'I think he may be in danger.'

'I hope you are wrong, for your own sake as well as his,' said Robert. 'We will have to deal with this by ourselves for now. We have no evidence, no proof of anything yet. Anyone we told would probably just laugh at us. In fact, I can't believe it's true. Let's forget about it until something happens.'

Felix was not very reassured, but had to agree that they had little to go on. He tried to put it out of his mind.

CHAPTER THREE

One day Master Thomas told Felix to go down to the shipyard to order a new mast and rigging rope for the *Gascogne,* the oldest of his ships. Felix loved the shipyards – the smell of canvas and rope and wood, the noise of saws, hammers and chisels at work. On this day Felix paused to admire two half-finished galleys, which were sitting on wooden props like two fat gulls on their nests. The men were busy shaping the hulls, forcing the wooden planks into a curve with a maze of ropes and stakes. Later, when they were happy with the shape of the galley, they would strengthen the body with a skeleton of wooden ribs on the inside of the hull. Then they would seal the joints with pitch to make them watertight. Felix wondered who would sail these ships, what cargo they would carry, what storms they would have to face in their lifetime. Once again, as he thought of storms, a sense of foreboding swept over Felix and he struggled to make sense of a swirling picture that filled his head. Then he shook off the gloomy feeling and went to speak to one of the men about his order.

'A new mast, you say?' said the clerk, looking worried.

'We'll do our best for Master Thomas, of course, but you can see how busy we are. The King has requested three galleys to be fitted out and sent to Portsmouth; he sails to France soon. Then there's the Flemish ships . . .'

'A new order from Flanders?' asked Felix.

'No, no. Repairs. You haven't heard the news, then? Pirates – English, they say – attacked the ships last night outside the harbour. They fired burning arrows into the sails and wounded several of the crew with their sword blows. Stole jewellery and cloth enough to fill their wretched barge, then fled into the night.'

First, Ralph's midnight outing, arguments, talk of owlers . . . now pirates. Was there any connection? Were Thomas de Bon or his ships in danger? Could the pirates be the men from Blythburgh that he and Robert had seen on Kings Holme beach? Felix walked back to the manor house engrossed, trying to fit all the pieces of a jigsaw puzzle together. He told Master Thomas about the delay on the mast, and asked him about the pirates.

'You mustn't worry, Felix. My ships are well-built and the crews are loyal, brave men. They will defend themselves well against an attack if need be.'

So once again, Felix tried to push his fears to the back of his mind. As the summer turned to autumn, he often spent his spare time with Robert, helping his family prepare for winter. They took the cow to the meadow to graze, and led the pigs into the woods to feed on the green acorns that would help to fatten them up before they were slaughtered. They collected wood for the fire and cut reeds from the marsh to mend the thatched roof. They planted vegetables in the cottage garden and mended the beehive. One day, they went to the heathland outside the town to gather heather to fill the mattresses. They took John Orford's wheat to the mill to be ground into flour. There was always something to be done to keep the family warm and fed.

Then one day it was time to repair the sea wall and strengthen it against the winter storms. Every household in the town sent one man each day to the shore until the work was done. One of the bailiffs organised them into gangs. One gang made up tight bundles of thin twigs, which they then stacked up in a long row all along the top of the shore. Others collected baskets of pebbles from near the harbour entrance, which they used to fill in the gaps between the twig bundles. The finished wall stretched for about two miles along the sea edge of Dunewic. The work went on from first light to dusk, day after day, but no one complained. They knew how important it was to keep the port free of shingle and to protect the houses that stood close to the water.

Robert and Felix worked side by side, chatting quietly.

'My father remembers a church that once stood on the seaward side of our cottage,' said Robert. 'The sea swept it away – and the land it stood on – before I was born.'

'A little wooden church with a thatched roof?' asked Felix in a strange voice.

'I don't know. Why?'

Felix remembered the picture of the little church that had come to him when he had looked down on the town from the tower on Cock Hill. It was a simple church, a special church, but not like any of those he had seen in Dunewic, with their carved stonework and rich stained-glass windows.

'What's the matter, Felix? You are quite pale all of a sudden.' Robert looked at his friend, but saw that there would be no answer. How often did his friend seem to slip into another, ghostly world, without warning. Robert usually tried to help him return to the real world by changing the subject.

'I'm looking forward to the Feast of St Leonard, aren't you?' he asked.

'What happens then?'

'Oh, Felix!' cried Robert, exasperated. 'The Fair of course. Three days, it lasts. The whole town is there, and traders come from Ely, Norwich . . . foreign merchants, too. There will be games and music, and travelling players. It's like a huge shopping party for the people of Dunewic!'

• • • • •

St Leonard's Fair began early on November 5th. A heavy sea mist hung damp over the town and the church bells – St Leonard's first, then St John's, St Nicholas' and all the others – clashed and clanged, calling everyone to mass. After the service the shopkeepers and craftsmen set up their stalls in the market square and waited for St John's bell to ring for trading to begin. Everything was there: from pots and pottery, glass and jewellery, tapestries and silks to fruit and vegetables, fresh bread, cheeses and wine. Shoemakers displayed all kinds of leather shoes, some decorated with embroidery, jewels or fur, from pointed slippers to long buttoned boots. Hatmakers were selling caps, bonnets and wide-brimmed hats. Horse traders led their animals into the town across Pales Dyke, where the mayor welcomed them to Dunewic. Once in the market square, every trader paid his dues to the bailiff's clerk and joined his voice to the chorus that cajoled the buying public to buy their wares. There were foreign voices to be heard, too. Rich merchants from France, Flanders and Italy had sailed into the port before the Fair, bringing wine, wool, furs and jewels to sell.

Felix found himself in the middle of the noisy, colourful scene, helping Ralph to set up a covered stall for Master Thomas. They covered the trestle table with a heavy red cloth and arranged samples of fabrics and furs. Casks of wine stood at one end, and baskets of salt at the other. Ralph was in a great hurry to be finished, and dashed away as soon as he could. Felix wondered, not for the first time, what Ralph's 'business' might be. When Master Thomas arrived, he sent Felix off to look round the Fair. He joined Robert and his mother, who were buying provisions for the winter: salt, spices, candles, some new clogs for Robert. Robert bought a set of wooden dice, and Felix chose a penknife with a carved bone handle, for sharpening his quill pens. The boys entered an archery competition and watched some youths fighting with long wooden staves.

The second day of the Fair seemed busier and noisier than the first. Felix acted as clerk at his Master's stall, writing down what goods had been sold, and the prices paid. From the stall he watched the new arrivals to Dunewic: musicians, jugglers and acrobats who would entertain the crowds and who, like all travelling people, brought news from near and far. Later in the day, Felix and Robert were able to watch a tightrope walker make his way gingerly across a rope strung across a side street. Dozens of people were gazing up, holding their breath in excitement, when a mob of drunken men rushed out of an ale house and ran down the street towards the spectators.

'Now – the thatch!' cried one of the mob, at which the leader hurled a flaming torch on to a roof. Within seconds the thatch was crackling and smoking.

'Quick – the poles! Water!' People in the crowd had one thought – to put out the fire before it spread to the other houses. Some found buckets of water to douse the flames, while others pulled the burning thatch down to the ground with long hooked poles.

Felix pulled at Robert's sleeve.

'It's them, the men from Blythburgh. The men on Kings Holme beach! Come on, we must warn Master Thomas.' The boys ran after the mob, who had headed off towards the market square. No one noticed another figure, no

stranger to Dunewic or Felix, slip quietly out of the ale house and disappear in the direction of Bridge Gate.

By the time the boys caught up with the rioters, they were causing havoc among the traders, pushing over stalls, jeering at the foreign merchants and sending animals flying. Few people tried to stop the gang. They were armed with knives and wooden staves, and too drunk to care what they did. They escaped down Bridge Street, leaving the townspeople to clear up the mess and resume business. Felix and Robert found Master Thomas surveying the mess at his stall. Silver pennies lay scattered on the ground, a basket lay on its side, the spilled salt soaking up the deep red wine that leaked from a gash in a cask. The boys helped to set things straight, but Felix could not hide his anger that Ralph was not there to help.

'Where is Master Ralph, sir?' he asked.

'He went to the ale house – said he had some business of his own to attend to. I let him go. Don't blame him for this,' replied Master Thomas.

'But . . . ' began Felix.

'No buts. I must go to the Guildhall to make my complaint to the bailiffs about this damage. Then it's business as usual. There have been riots before, my boy. Some people outside Dunewic are jealous of our wealth, but cannot find a way to beat us.'

'Those men were from Blythburgh, I'm sure of it,' said Felix.

'It's possible. But what makes you so certain?' said Master Thomas.

'It's a long story, sir.'

'Then its telling must wait until after the Fair. I will tell the bailiffs what you said. Others may have recognised them, too. Stay here until I get back, Felix.'

Felix watched his Master walk slowly across the market

squarc to the Guildhall, where other merchants and traders had already gathered to make statements about the riot. He wondered if he would be able to convince Master Thomas of his suspicions about Ralph, and his fear that the Master was in danger.

• • • • •

On the evening of the third and last day of the Fair, Thomas de Bon held a feast in the great hall of his house, to which other merchants and their wives were invited. The guests were dressed in rich robes of wine red, deep blue and emerald green, decorated with silver and gold thread and fur trimmings. They sat on the long benches either side of the oak table, on which the silver and pewter wine goblets sparkled in the candlelight. Ralph and Felix help to serve the food, as many as twelve different courses, from the apple and pear tart and roasted salmon to the almond omelette and spiced cakes. Each course was heralded by a fanfare, and the guests were entertained by minstrels' songs and a juggler's antics.

At first, Felix paid little attention to the conversations that rose and fell around him, but as he tended the fire he became aware that Ralph was paying close attention to Master Thomas and a French merchant.

'When will you come to my country then, Master Thomas?' asked the French merchant.

'The *Selig* will leave in a week's time. I will join her for this voyage,' replied Master Thomas. 'But I want to return to Dunewic for the start of the new year.'

'Then it is agreed,' replied his friend.'We will welcome you in Bordeaux before Christmas.'

Felix wondered why Ralph looked so pleased at this news. Did he want their Master out of the way? Why? Felix was afraid, but could not say what he feared might happen.

• • • • •

The night before Thomas de Bon was due to sail, he sent for Felix after supper, as he often did.

'Another game of chess, Master?' asked Felix.

'Not this evening, Felix. I have some important business to attend to before we sail tomorrow. Fetch your parchment and quill and inkhorn.'

When Felix was seated at the writing desk, Master Thomas looked at him kindly.

'Before you write, Felix, I want to explain what this document is for. I know you are concerned for my safety, and I know why. I also know that there is nothing you or I can do about it. But there is another danger, too, against which we are all powerless. The sea is our friend – and our enemy. It brings us wealth and wisdom from other lands, but it can take all that away and more when it is in angry mood. If anything should happen to me on this journey and I die, then I want you to have some of what I leave behind. Then when you are older you will be able to sail to foreign lands and perhaps make your fortune.

Ralph must have his share, but you have taken the place of my son who drowned and you shall be rewarded as one of my family.'

Felix was too stunned to work out what this might mean, or to make any reply to Master Thomas, who in any case started to dictate the document, setting out the part of his goods and wealth that would come to Felix on his death.

When it was finished, Master Thomas summoned two servants to make their mark as witnesses to his signature. When they had left he sealed the document by softening a piece of dark red wax in the flame of a candle and pressing into it his personal seal, showing three barrels and a sheep.

Then he placed the parchment in a carved wooden chest full of similar scrolls, locked it and gave the little iron key to Felix.

'Keep this with you always,' he said. 'It is the key to your future. May God protect you.'

Felix could not sleep that night. He prayed that Thomas de Bon would return to Dunewic safely and that the document he had just written would not see the light of day for many years to come. In the meantime, he was determined to keep an eye on Ralph, to spy if necessary, to find out why he was so pleased at Master Thomas's departure.

CHAPTER FOUR

Master Thomas sailed out of Dunewic harbour aboard the *Selig* on a bright, frosty morning in mid November. The North Sea was metal grey, flat and seemingly endless. The loaded galley sat low in the water, weighed down by its cargo of wool and grain bound for Flanders and France. The 56-strong crew had to row hard for an hour or more until they hit the wind and could raise the sail. Felix and Robert watched from Robert's garden until they could see the galley no more. Then Felix told Robert about the document and the key that now hung from his belt.

'From Master Thomas's hints, it sounds as though you may be right about Ralph after all,' said Robert. 'Perhaps it is time to look in St Peter's Church.'

'What for?' asked Felix.

'Some clue. He did go in there when you followed him on that first night, remember?'

So the boys went to the church. The air inside was damp and salty. They walked all round the edge, along the wall, but found few hiding places and no clues. Then

Robert stopped in the west chapel, where the sun was glinting off a brass plate on a knight's tomb. He knelt down and called Felix to read the inscription to him. As he put his knee on the corner of the brass, it gave way slightly and the opposite corner came up out of its stone setting. The boys looked at each other, wondering.

'If the gravestone is so loose,' said Felix, 'perhaps it has been disturbed recently. Perhaps there is something hidden underneath?'

'Yes, the body of a knight,' said Robert. 'I am not going to disturb a grave, even for you, Felix.'

Felix was not so easily put off the scent, however. Was it just a body? Or some awful secret that might lead him to Ralph? Felix squatted on his heels, closed his eyes tightly, just in case, and pulled gently at the raised corner of brass. It came away so easily that he nearly fell backwards.

'Hold this for me,' said Felix.

'That, and no more,' said Robert. 'This is the Devil's game.'

Holding his breath and peering through half closed eyes, Felix looked down into the tomb. No face. No bones. Only blackness.

'It's all right, Robert. It's too dark to see much, anyway. Fetch me a candle, please.' Felix was feeling brave all of a sudden. Robert held a lighted candle over the black hole in the ground. It flickered in the cold draught that came up from below, until he cupped his hand round it. As the flame burned steadier and stronger, the boys gasped.

There below them lay several wooden chests, some of them decorated in gold and silver, others carved or plain. This was no tomb, then. More a treasure trove. Felix jumped into the hole before Robert could stop him. He tried not to think of the mice and rats lurking in the corners as he tried each chest lid in turn. The first to open was full to the brim with silver pennies. Another was stuffed full of sailors clothes – Flemish, thought Felix. A third contained jewellery – silver brooches and clasps, gold bracelets and rings. Again, Felix saw from their design that they were not English. Were they perhaps the booty the pirates claimed from those Flemish ships that had been repaired in the shipyard? And was Ralph involved in any of this? Felix suddenly saw a way of finding out once and for all. He chose a smooth, round clasp and pinned it at the neck of his cloak, then he called to Robert to pull him out.

'Ssh!' replied Robert. 'Someone's coming . . . what shall we do?'

'Jump down into here,' whispered Felix. 'No one will see us. Quick!'

Robert decided he was more afraid of being caught than of the dark of the tomb, so he jumped. Felix stood on one of the chests to reach up and pull the brass plate over the hole, leaving a tiny gap for a sliver of light. They heard two men's voices.

'It's Ralph!' whispered Felix. Robert nodded, too frightened to speak. The men could be heard quite clearly now. They must be standing close to the knight's grave.

'He feels old,' Ralph was saying. 'I think he may not sail again. This may be the best chance we'll ever have. Are your men still looking for "work"?' he asked.

'You know that for the right fee they are always ready to follow orders,' said the other man.

'Good. They will be well paid. Our brave brass knight will see to that,' said Ralph, tapping his foot on the tombstone.

Felix clenched his fists as he waited for Ralph to see that the stone was out of place.

'When does Thomas return, then?' continued the other man.

'One week after Christmas was his plan. We will have to keep watch. You must be ready to go to sea at any time. When you get the signal, leave at once. I will cross to Kings Holme and wait for you at the usual place. It's well hidden from the port.'

'What about the boy?'

'I can keep Felix busy. He will be anxious to prepare a warm welcome for his precious Master. Don't concern yourself with him, you've got other matters to see to.'

'Blythburgh pirates at your service, my lord!' scoffed the man.

'This is no joking matter. Nor is it plain piracy. We take his life, but not his ship. Just make it *look* like the work of pirates, and make your getaway before anyone recognises you. You must collect your disguises before Christmas, but remember – if you speak during the attack, the Flemish clothes will not hide your identity. Now I must go. Wait a few minutes before leaving. I don't want us to be seen together.'

Felix found it difficult to stay calm and quiet. Now that he knew what Ralph's plan was he felt not fear but anger. As soon as the two men had gone, the boys climbed out of the tomb. Robert spoke first.

'I'm sorry, Felix, I should have believed you. You were right all the time. Now it is too late to do anything.'

'It's not too late. We must find a way to warn Master Thomas. Whatever he suspected of Ralph, I am sure it was not murder. He must be told of the danger he is in.'

'I can't see how we can do that when he is France. Come on, I'm frozen. Let's talk about it on the way home.'

When the boys parted, they were no nearer to finding a solution and agreed to meet again soon. Felix was deep in thought as he entered the manor house and was puzzled when Ralph shouted, 'Where did you get that, boy?'

'What? Oh this . . .' Felix had quite forgotten the silver clasp pinned to his cloak. He should have removed it, since he no longer needed proof of Ralph's involvement with the pirates. How was he going to explain it away without arousing Ralph's suspicions?

'The clasp, you mean?' Felix tried to sound surprised. 'Master Thomas gave it to me before he left – I think he bought it from one of those Flemish merchants who dined here after the Fair.'

'That sounds odd. Why should he give you anything at all? Tell me, boy.'

'It was a Christmas present, because he will still be away on the 25th, that's all.'

Would Ralph accept his story?

'So, Felix. A present for the new boy but nothing for his loyal servant Ralph? I might have known . . .'

'Perhaps he will bring back something more special for you from France at New Year,' suggested Felix, who was feeling quite pleased with his story of Christmas presents.

'Yes, well, we'll all get unexpected presents at New Year, boy, never fear,' said Ralph. Felix felt his confidence sucked away by the thought of what Ralph really meant, but at least he had managed to put Ralph off the scent for the moment.

CHAPTER FIVE

Felix was kept very busy in the days leading up to Christmas. Ralph sent him on errands to the blacksmith, the shipwright, and the warehouses. He even sent him to the leper hospital to deliver some chickens and salted pork.

'The Master always likes to send them a gift at Christmas. No reason why it should be different this year. Next year . . .' Felix felt a wave of panic flood over him as he realised how little time was left to stop Ralph's plan succeeding. He went to find Robert, and they walked along the sea wall, talking it over. An icy wind blew in off the grey-brown water. The tide was in, the waves swirling and crashing against the barricade of wood and stone. Felix tried to picture another port, on the Atlantic, where the *Selig* waited to set sail for home.

'It is foolish to think we can do anything about this by ourselves,' said Robert. 'I think we should tell my father.'

John Orford listened patiently to their story and to the boys' relief took it seriously. After some thought he told them that the only solution was to tell the crew of the patrol boat that sailed up and down the coast near Dunewic on the lookout for pirates.

'If they can spot the Blythburgh boat before it reaches the *Selig*, then Master Thomas will be safe, but his is not the only ship they have to protect, so we must let them know if we suspect Ralph is about to make a move. You must keep a close watch on his movements, Felix,' said John Orford. Felix was glad that someone else was making the decisions.

'What about me, Father?' asked Robert. 'I want to help too.'

'There is work for you too, Robert, don't worry. If Master Thomas planned to return by New Year's Day, that's two days away. He will be on his way already. From now on, you must spend as much time as possible in the conde tower, as though you were watching for the fish.'

'But I will be watching for the *Selig*!' cried Robert.

'Yes, of course. Ralph must have a secret lookout post on the cliffs, but the tower is higher than any land round here. You should spot the *Selig* before he does. Remember that it will appear down the coast, from the south. Any ships from the east are probably Flemish trading ships.'

'What if it's dark when it arrives?' asked Felix.

'A galley that size would only enter our narrow harbour by daylight,' replied John Orford. 'Now. I must alert the patrol boat. Then we must pray that the pirates are caught in time.'

The next two days were very difficult for Felix. Ralph became increasingly short-tempered.

'Stop following me round everywhere,' he said. 'And stop looking so anxious. Your concern for your Master is most touching, but you must grow up and accept the dangers of the sea.'

'What dangers do you mean?' asked Felix.

'Anything can happen at sea. Perhaps, even now, he is caught in a storm, shipwrecked on the rocks of Brittany. Or stranded in fog in the Channel. Or trapped by foreign pirates . . .' Felix was not surprised at this. It would suit Ralph very well if everyone believed that the *Selig* was attacked by chance by unknown men. How was all this nightmare going to end, he wondered?

Two days later there was still no sign of the *Selig*. How much longer could he expect his friends to stay on the alert, thought Felix. Perhaps Ralph was right, after all, and an accident had befallen his Master and crew. He lay on his mattress, unable to sleep, and thought back to all the evenings he had spent with Master Thomas, talking and playing chess. Chess! That's what he would do to pass the time. He crept out of the room where Ralph lay snoring, and felt his way in the dark to the room above the great hall. Felix settled down by the hearth where a log still burned gently, throwing out a little warmth and light.

'. . . and if black takes that white pawn, the black knight can move here to put the king in check. Then the white bishop . . .'

'What do you think you're playing at?' Felix's hand froze round the piece of ivory at the sight of Ralph in the doorway, a ghostly figure in the light of his candle.

'I couldn't sleep,' whispered Felix, afraid of this man and his cruel temper.

'How can you expect to sleep when you are not in your bed? How dare you leave your room and go wandering round this house which is not yours? Get back at once!'

Felix did as he was ordered. He lay down once again on the rough mattress and reached down for the sheepskin blanket. As he did so he realised he was still clutching a chess piece. He pushed it into his tunic pocket. He would return it in the morning. He prayed that tomorrow, finally, his Master would return and that he and his friends could thwart Ralph's plans once and for all. As Felix fell asleep to dream of dark tombs and angry seas, Ralph wearily pulled on his leggings and winter boots, drew on his sword belt and left the house.

• • • • •

'Felix, wake up! It's time! Come on!' Robert shook his friend awake. Felix sat up, startled, and struggled to shake off his dreams.

'The *Selig* – I think she's on her way. You must come.'

Felix found it hard to believe that after all the waiting, Master Thomas was there, in sight of Dunewic.

'Who let you in?' asked Felix. 'Have you told the patrol – and your father? How long ago was it?

'The stable boy – yes, yes – half an hour ago,' said Robert, answering each question in turn. 'Now it's my turn. Where's Ralph?'

Felix looked over at the empty bed.

'I don't know. He must have left early.'

'Well, we mustn't waste time here. Let's go down to the port.'

The sea and sky seemed to run into each other, both the same flat grey colour.

'It might snow today,' said Robert. 'It's got much colder since first light.'

Felix realised that his friend had been on guard in the tower while he had slept.

'Can you see her now? I can't,' said Felix.

The boys scanned the open space but could see no sails, although several small boats were moving in and out of the harbour and a barge was visible further out.

'That might be the patrol boat,' said Robert.

'Or the Blythburgh boat,' said Felix. 'But where's the *Selig*?'

'Hidden round a headland down the coast, I expect. She'll come into view again later.'

Felix felt too cold and restless just to stand by the shore waiting.

'Let's go over to Kings Holme,' he said. ' We can find out if Ralph and his men have spotted her yet.'

Robert was not keen to trek across the marshy wasteland on such a miserable day. He knew that the pools of water hidden beneath the reeds would be icy cold and that the dunes would give little protection if the wind grew any stronger. He tried to dissaude Felix, but Felix was determined and threatened to go alone, so Robert relented.

'Very well. We must find the ferry man.'

The ferry man agreed reluctantly to take them across.

'What the devil draws you to such a place on a day like this? The weather's turning, that's for sure,' he grumbled.

Once they landed on the marsh, the boys headed into the wind and made for the dunes. Felix wondered what he expected to see. Whatever it was, would it make any difference? They scrambled to the top of the dunes and looked up and down the pebble beach. Nothing! No boat. No men. Then suddenly Robert pulled on Felix's sleeve.

'Look!' he cried, pointing away to his left. 'A fire. They were here all right.'

In a strange way, Felix was reassured by a pile of drift-wood and the smouldering embers of an abandoned fire, now threatened by the incoming tide. He decided it was time to return to the mainland.

As they recrossed the narrow channel leading into the harbour, the prow of the little rowing boat rose and fell sharply as it cut across the racing waves.

'That's a bad sea on its way, I reckon,' said the ferry man.

Felix seemed to consider the weather for the first time.

'The wind will blow the *Selig* home faster, but it will slow the patrol boat down,' he said.

'It won't help the Blythburgh boat either, though,' Robert pointed out.

By the time the boys reached Robert's house the sky had turned inky blue and the sea was surging furiously towards the coast. Ribs of white foam fanned out from the shore and, further out, the water rose in menacing sheets that curved at the top and then collapsed, to be replaced by others, yet stronger.

'There'll be no fishing until the storm is spent, so we'll have to settle down and wait,' said Robert's father.

'But the *Selig*!' cried Felix.

'She's many times bigger than my litle fishing boat, and her cargo will make her sit low in the water, less exposed to the wind and waves. In any case, she's weathered winter storms these twenty years past. She'll survive this one.'

'What about the patrol boat?'

'Depends – they might have turned back by now, but if not, they might have trouble.'

A few hours later it was clear to everyone in the town that this was not to be just another winter storm. It was almost dark, although not yet evening, and the noise of the storm made it difficult to think clearly. The wind howled, tearing at the thatched roofs and scattering debris all around. Windmill sails spun furiously, white against black. Waves loomed out of the darkness, sharp in the flashes of lightning, and charged at Dunewic like serried ranks of soldiers bent on destruction.

The older people of Dunewic had witnessed such storms before. They knew it was only a matter of time before the sea wall would have to let the water in. John Orford knew that his house could soon be flooded, and those of his neighbours too. He would have to move his family to higher ground, taking the animals and bedding with them. Felix knew now that he was helpless to rescue Master Thomas, whose battle would be with the forces of nature and not any pirates, and that he must help this family who had been so ready to help him.

'You must take shelter in Thomas de Bon's house,' he said. 'The animals can go in the stables.'

A deep rumble, very close, interrupted him. The ground shook as though hit by an earthquake. Everyone hurried to the doorway and looked towards the harbour mouth. The far end of the sea wall had been sucked away, swallowed by the sea, leaving the base of a windmill and the first house on the very edge of dry land. As the waves ate away at the sandy ground, the windmill swayed, then collapsed in slow motion, the planks of wood swirling away on the water like fallen leaves. There was a pause as the sea seemed to draw breath, then the muddy water poured on to the land, soaking everything in its path and spreading out in a dark stain.

Felix and Robert looked at each other, aghast. John Orford and his wife told the boys what to collect – cooking pan, wooden bowls, animal skins, a basket of fish, bread, boots and clogs. They put the chickens in a basket with a lid and made a rope harness for the cow. Robert led out the two pigs. At last they were ready to go.

There was no time to lose. As the family faced the storm, the sea wall broke just behind their house and within seconds salt water was rushing over the doorstep and lifting the strewn rushes off the ground. In the street, other fishing families joined them on the same sad, desperate journey. At first, they kept looking back. Then it became too painful to watch as other houses followed the first into a watery grave. But there was a moment when the whole procession halted, shocked by a sudden crashing of stone.

'It's the church!' cried Felix. The heavy stone tower of St Leonard's church disappeared before their eyes. Beyond, the ships in the harbour, normally so well protected, were rolling and tipping wildly, the wooden hulls groaning and splintering as they were hurled against the harbour wall. Felix wondered what had become of the *Selig*, out at sea. Was that in splinters too?

CHAPTER SIX

Several families took shelter in Master Thomas's house, yet despite the number of people, a terrible quietness contrasted with the roar of the gale. The animals had been settled, children comforted, simple meals prepared and shared. Bedding and rugs were drying out by the huge fire and some people were already trying to sleep. There was little to be done until the storm had exhausted itself.

Felix was busy trying to help people in any way he could, when the stable boy called his name.

'What is it?' he asked.

'It's – something awful. Come to the stable yard. Quickly!' The stable boy, usually so strong and confident, looked pale and shaken.

'Look!' said the boy, pointing to a long dark shape on the ground. 'Two men brought him up, and ran off. I don't know who they were,' and he started to cry.

Felix knelt down beside the body, which was wrapped in a rough cloth, soaked through and smelling of the sea. Was this the news he had been dreading for so long? Was it to end like this, after all? Had his master drowned in the storm, like his son? Or – worse – had Ralph caught up with him and murdered him while the sea roared round them? Felix thought sadly of the man who had put so much trust in him. And if his master was dead, how could he, a boy, stand up to Ralph alone? The stable boy touched him on the shoulder, bringing him back to the present.

'Hold the lantern steady,' said Felix, as he pulled back the cloth.

Oh, thank God, thought Felix, sobbing with relief, for it was not Master Thomas but Ralph who lay lifeless on the ground.

'How did he die?' asked the stable boy.

'We'll probably never know,' said Felix, 'unless the two men who brought him tell us how they found him.' Felix doubted that they would ever find out the truth but as he tried to puzzle out what might have happened, he realised that there was still a chance that Master Thomas might get home safely, after all. He went back into the great hall and told John Orford what had happened.

'It's a terrible end to anyone's life, yet there is a kind of justice in it,' he said. 'And perhaps there will be better news in the morning, who knows?' Felix could tell by his tone of voice that he did not really believe the *Selig* would survive the night.

'We must all try to sleep now,' continued Robert's father. 'There will be much to do when the storm stops. The harbour mouth must be kept clear – if it is blocked by sand and shingle dragged there by the sea, the fishing boats will not get through, let alone a galley.'

Once again, Felix found himself unable to sleep. In the end he left the hall, took a dry cloak and boots and went into the street. If only the wind would drop, he thought, but he was swept along in its path, past St Peter's church and down towards the port. When Felix reached Cock Hill he moved round until he was out of the wind, and without thinking began to climb the turf steps to the bottom of the tower. As soon as he started up the ladder, the force of the wind hit him again, but he clung on, driven upwards almost against his will. He had to get to the top, to see for himself, before it was too late . . .

• • • • •

Felix stood on the top of the tower. The wind dropped suddenly, and Dunewic lay below him, eerie in the stillness, lit up by the moon. All around, houses stood with black holes where their roofs had been, their thatch swept aside by the wind. A half-finished galley lay shipwrecked on dry land in the shipyard. Barrels and baskets were strewn all along the quay, dragged out of the warehouses. But when Felix looked round to check on the sea wall, he could not make sense of what he saw, for not only had the sea wall crumbled away, so too had many of the houses that had stood behind it. St Leonard's church had gone, and several windmills. Felix felt his eyes fill with tears at the thought of all the years of work that had been swept away in a few careless hours of the storm.

He wiped his sleeve over his face, wet with tears, salt spray and rain.

It was then that he saw the sail, ghostly pale and ragged, moving across the sea. Felix flung himself at the top of the ladder and put his foot out into the darkness. Before he could find the top rung a sudden, unearthly roar filled his ears and the wind, full of a new and terrible energy, lifted his cloak and whipped it across his face, blinding him. He reached up with one hand to pull the cloak away and the wind, seeing its chance, tore at him so that his other hand was not strong enough to hold him on the ladder. Felix knew, as he fell away into the blackness, that this was how it was to end.

• • • • •

When Felix awoke, he sat forward, his back sore from leaning against the dinghy. He looked ahead of him at the flat sea, calm in the late afternoon sun. A little red-sailed sailing boat came into view over the horizon. Felix felt his heart race. Had he fallen? Was the storm over? Where was he? This was not Dunewic. This was – Dunwich village. Felix felt a mixture of relief and disappointment seep through him. Had it all been a dream? It had all seemed so real – Robert, Ralph, Master Thomas . . .

He stood up slowly and turned sadly away from the sea, past the fishing huts and back up St James's Street. As he passed the little museum, he heard voices. He stepped inside.

'And this is what Dunwich looked like in the Middle Ages, before the great storm of 1286.' The curator was showing his visitors a large model of a town. Felix looked.

'Yes, that's right!' he said. 'There's Master Thomas's house, and the conde tower on Cock Hill and . . .' He looked up and saw faces peering at him oddly. He stopped. He knew that feeling of knowing while others round him seemed from another world, full of suspicion.

'Sorry,' he said, and moved away, pretending to look at the wall displays. A word, his name, caught his eye. He read:

'. . . Bishop Felix, from Bordeaux in France, arrived in Dunwich in 630. He was made Bishop of East Anglia and lived here for seventeen years, until his death. He built a church . . .'

Felix ran out into the sunshine, his head buzzing with words and pictures all muddled up. Felix . . . France . . . Dunewic . . . A dream? Of course, yet . . .

The sea wind was gathering force again. Felix walked briskly up towards the ruins of the medieval leper hospital. He stood looking at the stone arch of Middle Gate, and plunged his hands into his pockets. His right hand felt a pebble, smooth and cold. He drew it out, trying to remember where he had picked it up. He opened his hand. There, on his palm, lay a piece of yellow-white ivory, the bishop from a chess set.